THE WATCHMAN'S FLUTE

The Watchman's Flute

JOHN HEATH-STUBBS

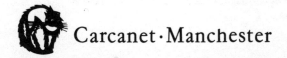

Carcanet · Manchester

Acknowledgements:

Some of these poems have appeared in *Penguin Modern Poets* number 20; *Satires & Epigrams* (Tunnel Books); *Four Poems in Measure* (Helikon Press, New York); *Poems for Shakespeare* 4 (Globe Playhouse), and in the following periodicals: *Poetry Review, The Observer, Broadsheet* (Dublin), *The Cremorne Review, The Scotsman, Gallery, Cracked Looking Glass, Aquarius, Atlantic Review, PN Review, Windows, Lapis Lazuli, Frontier, The Tablet, Agenda, Ishmael, Poetry & Audience* and *Two Rivers.*

The translations from the Greek Anthology were done in collaboration with Carol A. Whiteside and appeared in *The Greek Anthology* (Allen Lane). 'Quetzalcoatl' and 'Old Mobb' make free use of material from Irene Nicholson's *Fireflies in the Night* (Faber) and Wendy Boase's *The Folklore of Hampshire and the Isle of Wight* (Batsford) respectively.

First published in 1978
Second Impression 1979 by
Carcanet New Press Limited
330-332 Corn Exchange
Manchester M4 3BG

The publisher acknowledges the financial assistance of the Arts Council of Great Britain.

Printed in Great Britain by Unwin Brothers Ltd., Old Woking

CONTENTS

6

TO THE QUEEN

on the occasion of Her Majesty's Silver Jubilee, 1977

Because the heart is finite, and can give
Its love and loyalty only to particulars—
Seeing in the known village, city, country,
A partial revelation of that one good place
Where all the just are citizens—I frame this dithyramb,
I plait this garland, for you, dynastic Elizabeth,
Presiding, with the sceptre that the dove tips,
Over your tidy, untidy, united kingdom
Where liberty still survives.

I twine the rose of England, blood-red and white,
The purple, aggressive thistle of Scotland, and
The green and gritty leek (St David's frugal dinner),
Also the shamrock, by which St Patrick,
Rather oddly, expounded the Trinity.
With these I would deck your doorposts.

Squalls buffet Britain, the off-shore ship of Europe;
She is driven to the Goodwins. Her sails are tattered and tatty,
Her masts split, her shrouds in shreds—and through them
Ill-omened fulmars and kittywakes skitter and glide.

Through a gap in the cloud-wrack I glimpse the mortal moon,
That first Elizabeth, augustly enthroned.
She shifts and changes: now she's the young
And golden-buskined Belphoebe, and now in her wane,
A raddled icon, her visage pitted and cratered.
At her side Magnificence, like the Lord Leicester,
Disperses golden angels to the groundlings—
Not for us neo-Elizabethans:

Economics, the law of the household, decrees
Dame Parsimony, the hard-faced lady cook,
Should have a finger in our festive pie—and yet

Let the silver trumpets of jubilee sound forth
Throughout the length and breadth of the land, to authorize
Judicious binge and beano—let bunting
Wave in the rain, in the cooling breezes of June, and let
                                                    there be
Cakes and real ale, bowling for the pig,
Folk-dancing, gilbertandsullivan, and all the other
Silly and beautiful things that signalize
A lasting and loyal love.

PURKIS

The red king lay in the black grove:
The red blood dribbled on moss and beech-mast.

With reversed horseshoes, Tyrrel has gone
Across the ford, scuds on the tossing channel.

Call the birds to their dinner. 'Not I,' said the hoarse crow,
'Not I,' whistled the red kite
'Will peck from their sockets those glazing eyes.'

Who will give him to his grave? 'Not I,' said the beetle
'Will shift one gram of ground under his corpse,
Nor plant in his putrid flank my progeny.'

Robin, red robin, will you in charity
Strew red Will with the fallen leaves?

'I cover the bodies of Christian men:
He lies unhouseled in the wilderness,
The desolation that his father made.'

Purkis came by in his charcoal-cart:
'He should lie in Winchester. I will tug him there—
Canons and courtiers perhaps will tip me,
A shilling or two for the charcoal-burner.'

Purkis trundled through the town gates,
And 'Coals!' he cried, 'coals, coals, coals,
Coals, charcoal, dry sticks for the burning!'

THE TWELVE LABOURS OF HERCULES

The Nemean Lion

To strangle a lion with one's bare hands:
This legitimates his kingship,
His godship. Hereafter
He wears the skin. We kill
What we love. We become
That which we kill.

The Lernaean Hydra

Foetid snake of the green, standing pool:
Nine heads—when one's cut off
Three others grow. Thus error
Pullulates. This kind
Is cauterized by fire.

The Cretan Bull

Bull of the earthquake—he stamps,
A city collapses; he bellows,
A tall tower tumbles.

The Erymanthean Boar

This blatant beast—
Grubber up of boundaries, snorting
Consumer of rations,
Defiler of the sweet meadow:
Catch him alive!

The Augean Stables

I cannot shift it.
Corruption, age-encrusted.
I cannot shift it. Water
From melting snows—turn on
The rivers like taps.

The Stymphalian Birds

Birds of the pestilent marsh, moulting
Darts of malaria, arrows
Of the swamp-fever. Bring pan and copper kettle:
Bang, bang, bang—
Be off, you scruffy puttocks!

The Arcadian Stag

The silver stag, proud-tined,
Fleeting over the white snow,
Through glassy winters. Let no spear-point
Graze his flank, no arrow-tip
Impugn with blood-drop. The Lady
Of Wild Things, with gossamer moonlight
Gathered about her body, loves him.
He's not for you.

The Horses of Diomede

Horses of the King of Thrace,
Of the northern war-lord. They are armour plated,
Jet powered, electronic brained.
In War's smoky manger
Man is their mashed provender.

The Girdle of Hippolyta

Man-woman, queen
Of the women without men.
Putrid scalps dangle from her waist;
She has burned away her right breast, she brayed
Her first-born boy-child in a mortar.
How to snatch the girdle
Of her steeled and homicidal chastity?

The Oxen of Geryon

A three-bodied giant, the sun
At morning, noon and evening.
Herdsman of the western shore, his cattle
The sunset clouds—such riches
Are for the taking.

The Apples of the Hesperides

These two, apples
Of man's remembered innocence,
Burning through the twilight dream, and guarded
By female voices and the watchful snake.
Recover them.

Cerberus

We all come down to this—
The yapping guard-dog of the final dungeon.
But bring your honey-cake,
The kneaded dough-ball of all your senses loved
In the bright day, up in the cheerful air.

THE DEATH OF LLEW

Under a shelter of withies,
Having bathed, getting out of the cauldron,
His trousers put on, one foot
On the back of a colt; a spear
Forged only at the sacring of the Mass—

Neither indoors nor outdoors,
Neither naked nor clothed,
Neither afoot nor on horseback;
A spear no Christian could make:

'Whizz!' sang the spear;
The flower-bride enchantingly synthesized
From maybloom, trefoil, broom, meadowsweet,
Turned to a boding owl; the hero's soul
Flew off, a verminous eagle.

For us also, somewhere
There waits the treacherous moment,
And waits the spear.

VOLUND

(on first looking into Auden's and Taylor's Edda*)*

I had read the tale before, and thought it
A catalogue of mythological horrors. But now I read it again
And know the significance. And I wonder
What craftsman-smith, captive or thrall,
Amid the violence of the Viking age,
In the bitterness of his heart
Devised this savage fable.

Through Murk Wood they flew, three girls,
Triple and identical, in swanfeather dress
Whistling through the bare branches, to sojourn
Nine seasons of love. Then they departed.

'We will ride to the ends of the earth,
To East and South, to seek them!' But Volund remained,
Lonely in Wolfdale, forging rings
Of red gold, waiting her return.

He counted his rings. One was missing. He dreamed
She had come back. When he next woke
He found himself in fetters; lamed,
Relegated to an island, forced to work
At trumpery trinkets.

'All shall be told, all:
The bodies of your boys
Lie under the blood-stained bellows; I have debauched
Your daughter to a drunken slut. But now I rise
On swan's wings. I am the Lord of the Elves,
Riding the cloudless air.'

(As Dionysus, also,
Over the house of Pentheus.)

So they think they can hamstring the artist, do they—
Sever his sinews, dissever him from his Muse?

QUETZALCOATL

Then he came to the unlimited, the luminous sea;
Behind him the desert where the coyote
Howled and the lizard basked;
Tree-size cylindrical cacti, volcanic cones
And the jagged line of mountains, in their hearts
Gold, jade, emeralds, petrol, silver.

He looked into the glass. He said:
'They have taken away my beauty and my power;
I shall not be loved or obeyed.'
So he put on his comely robe
Of trogon feathers, crossed over the breast;
And his turquoise mask, spotted with yellow;
He reddened his lips, and picked out
The serpent's teeth in red.

He said: 'My heart
Is the manic heart of Monteczuma, broken
By the flung stone; my power
The ruthlessness of Cortez, the anger
And justice of Juarez, the abstract order of Diaz,
The fury of Villa, and Maximilian
Silent before the firing-squad.
I suffer with the peons scraping the hard soil,
With the workers on the haciendas, and the itinerant
Fruit-pickers of California.

'I am tricked with phenomena, the fantasies
Of pulque and mescal—delusions
Of my mother the Serpent-skirted, the black
Virgin of Guadalupe; of my sister,
The Flower-bride, of Marina—
She who betrayed her people, the madness of Carlota
Dabbling her fingers in the Pope's cocoa, scalding
Her arm in the nuns' broth.'

Then all the birds came to say goodbye:
The scarlet macaw, the blue-jay,
The dove, the thrush, and the quail,
The gilded parrots with their human tongues,
The curasow with his malachite bill,
The tinamou brooding her burnished eggs,
The condor gliding with untwitching wings
Under the blood-drinking sun, the occellated
Turkey gobbling from the ground,
The motmot with his gnawed, racket feathers,
The colibri, darting in and out
Of the nectarous flower-bells—all
Whistled, whispered and grided farewell.

'Fire must purge'. He constructed the pyre.
The flames licked up,
The green robe frizzled, the mask cracked;
The body crumbled to white dust
Drifting on the desert wind.
But the heart rose up, a chalice
Filled with beating blood,
A crimson butterfly flapping skyward
Like a red flag.
It became the morning star,
Gleaming down from the mask above
Over the landscape of pain.

BEVIS OF HAMPTON

(For Norman Nicholson)

Bevis waded ashore through the surf
Of four-tided Solent. At his heels
The delicate island was glimpsed,
Unglimpsed, through the mist:
Victoria watches the yachts
Flit to and fro, decrees
Tea and biscuits in the library
For Mr Gladstone, invites
Mr Disraeli to stay for dinner.

Bevis—his bones were chalk and his flesh was clay,
The crest of his helm
Royal and Roman Winchester;
Arthur's table,
An amulet, hung on his brow.
Gorse and fern of the New Forest
The scrubby hair on his chest and groin.

As his feet touched the shingle and undercliff, coltsfoot.
Rest-harrow, scabious and knapweed
Blossomed about them—the Dartford warbler,
Stonechat and sand-martin spluttered a welcome.
Ponies obsequiously trotted forward—
They would convoy him inland.

'I am Bevis,' he shouted, 'I am Beow the barley-man.
I have been killing dragons and things
In the Middle East, now I come home
To claim my inheritance.'

His mouth was Southampton Water, where ships of Tarshish,
All the big steamers, chugged in and out, their holds
Bursting with biscuits you nibble, and beefsteaks.
Out of that throat the hymns of Isaac Watts
Arose in salutation to God and to judgement.

Miss Austen observed his coming
From the corner of her eye; on his shoulder, the down of
Selbourne—
There a retiring cleric discriminated the songs
Of willow-wren, chiffchaff, wood-wren.

Bevis—his right hand rested on Pompey and the great guns;
His left hand gently fondled
The dusty, fairy pavilions of Bournemouth.
In frozen horror a landlady
Stared at the ceiling, a spreading stain—
The blood of Alec D'Urberville.

The corner of his left sleeve
Lightly brushed the blue-slipper clay
Of the Barton beds, where eocene fossils
Attested a former sub-tropical climate,
And curled asleep, in his middle-class room, a boy
Surmised he might be a poet.

OLD MOBB

(i)

Old Mobb stood on the Romsey road:
A splendid equipage came along—
Inside was the Duchess of Portsmouth, with two French
footmen,
And two sleek and pampered spaniels.
'Fellow,' she said, 'do you know who I am?'
'Yes, and what you are—
You are the king's whore, I think,
And not kind Protestant Nellie, neither.'
'Villain, do you dare to touch me there!'
'Now I command where the king asks his favours.'
Said Old Mobb, politely removing
Three hundred pounds, a little gold watch,
And a very splendid string of pearls.

(ii)

Old Mobb was on the road at midnight:
Mercury, patron of thieves, swung in its orbit.
Came ambling by on an old grey mare
Mr John Gadbury the astrologer.
'I am a poor man, a poor scholar,
Pray you, spare me.' 'What you—
Who lease out the seven stars for hire
To cozen noodles. These golden chimers
And these silver chinkers make better music
Than all the circling spheres, and much more audible.'
Said Old Mobb, as he pocketed them.
'You cannot rob me of my skill,' said Gadbury,
'In physiognomy, and from your favour
I read you born for hanging.'

(iii)

Came trotting along on a neat black pony
Dr Cornelius Tilburgh,
Successful physician, with a bedside manner,
'Have you no care,' said he, 'for those
Your depradations ruined?'
'You with your clysters and blisters, your nostrums and
                                                boluses
Ruin more men than the cataracts of Nile.
Here, doctor, is a leaden pill—
Cough up, or void your superfluity:
No antidote, you know, for gunpowder.'
Said Old Mobb, as he extracted
Twenty-five pounds and a bright medal
With the king's own face upon it.

(iv)

A proud coach rumbled along
On the road towards the Winchester Assizes.
Judge Jeffreys stuck his head out of the window—
His great full wig, his brazen blotchy face:
'The law has claws and I incorporate the law.
Don't think, my man, that you'll escape from justice.'
'Though I shall dance on Tyburn, and you
Rot in the Tower, awaiting trial—
Yet there's another Judge we both must go to.
Who will fare better at those final sessions—
The Lord Chief Justice of England, he who hanged
Many poor men of the West at their own doorposts,
And doomed Dame Alice for her mere compassion
To broken fugitives, or a plain man of Hampshire
Who knew no master but his poverty?
Though he brandished a gun he never killed any
And prayed often
For God's forgiveness, even while he robbed,
As now I do.' said Old Mobb
Suiting the prigging action to the word.

SQUIRLING

When the red nutkin, the rufous shadow-tail,
And not the grey American immigrant,
Danced in the branches of the lady larch, or scolded
Down from the beech tree boughs—this was,
By tradition, a Hampshire sport.

Two weights joined by a leather strap,
Sharply hurled, could bring the squirrel down.

'Barbarous?' the enquirer asked. 'Well,' said the old forester,
'At least we do eat the squirrel
Which is more than the gentry does the fox.'

TO KEEP AWAY MOLES

(for Elspeth Barker)

Avaunt, mouldywarp,
    Out of my acres;
Vacate, velvet-coat,
    Your oubliettes and galleries;
The glebe of my neighbour
    Be for your pioning,
And my sward undisturbed:
    His earthworms are more succulent,
    His wire-worms more esculent,
    His leatherjackets of more nutriment.

That is the score,
Insectivore!

THE STAG BEETLES

'Cor, aren't they horrible! Where do they live?'—
The Cockney lady in the Insect House
At the London Zoo, standing by a case
Containing stag beetles, in a simulated habitat
Of twigs and oak-leaves. 'In the country.'
Replied her friend. I think that she conceived of
Civilized London surrounded by a vast
Primeval forest, known as 'the country'—
A dank, dark jungle, full of monstrous insects,
Waving their menacing jaws.
It is a vision I rather tend to share.

JANKYNMASS

(For Charles Causley)

Gnashing his teeth in the nether ice
    Wicked Jankyn lies,
While North East winds, unseasonably,
    Blemish our springtide skies.

The apple-blossom and the pear-blossom
    Are shivered from the spray,
While the hell-brewed frosts of Jankynmass
    Deflower the English May.

Bad Jankyn, he was a brewer
    Who brewed on a large scale;
From Havant westward to Penzance
    Men knew of Jankyn's ale,

And supped it down. And I am sure
    That it did them no harm—
Nor soap made froth, nor alum crude
    Had clarified the barm,

Nor what gave body to the brew
    Was any old dead rats,
Or poor half starved apprentice boys
    Who tumbled in the vats,

Befuddled by the heady fumes.
    (And surely envious sin
Gripped those who hinted, in their cups,
    That Jankyn pushed them in.)

But beer is a Teutonic drink
    That clouds the Saxon brain:
The peasants of the western shires
    Have a strong Celtic strain.

The Druid apple's their delight,
    Cider their *vin du pays*:
For this the bridal blossoming orchards
    Make beautiful the May—

A pleasant sight to bless men's eyes;
    Yet did not Jankyn bless—
The more the cider-sellers gain,
    The brewer profits less.

'Curse on the ungrateful jumblejuice,
    The pixy tanglefoot,
Curse on all ciders, sweet or dry,
    And applejack to boot;

'Grant me three nights of frost in May
    To blast the apple flower,
And my eternal soul I'll put
    For ever in your power!'

Old Nick, who's always somewhere around,
    Splashed out of Jankyn's tun,
With parchment, pen, and sealing wax,
    'Sign here!' he shouted, 'Done!'

Three North East winds, and three sharp frosts
    In the third week of May
He granted for bad Jankyn's sake,
    Until the Judgement Day,

To blight the christened apple-trees—
    But then he claimed his price
And clawed that stark, teeth-chattering soul
    Down to the nether ice.

SIMCOX

Simcox was one of several rather uninteresting
Ghosts, which popular report affirmed
Haunted the precincts of the College where
I had the privilege of my education.
A Junior Fellow (exactly in what field
His tedious studies ran was not remembered),
Simcox, it seems, was drowned—the Long Vacation
Of 1910, or '12, or thereabouts,
Somewhere off the coast of Donegal:
If accident or suicide I don't recall. But afterwards
Simcox began to manifest himself
In his old rooms, sitting in his large arm-chair,
With dripping clothes, and coughing slightly.
Simcox was wet in life, and wet in death.

To save embarrassment, it was decided
This should in future be the chaplain's room.
The chaplain of my day, a hearty
Beer-swilling extravert, and not much given—
Or so I would suppose—to exorcism,
Never, to my knowledge, did in fact aver
He had encountered Simcox. And anyway
Those visitings grew fainter with the years.
Simcox was dim in life, and dim in death.

A CROW IN BAYSWATER

A carrion crow flew over Bayswater—
Dews of morning distilled on his dark wings.

Shadows of night retired—the ghost
Of Peter Rachman, pursued
By phantom Alsatian dogs,
Scurried down St Stephen's Gardens.

He sailed over All Saints Church, and Father Clark
Unlocking the door for Anglican Eucharist;

Over spilling dustbins, where
Warfarin-resistant mice
Licked the insides of empty soup-cans,
Worried
Potato peelings, stale sliced bread.

'Cark!' said the crow, a raucous croak—to me
The stern music of freedom—

'I will go to Kensington Gardens;
Down by the Round Pond.
New-hatched ducklings are out:
We'll scrag a couple for breakfast.'

HORNBILLS IN NORTHERN NIGERIA

(To Hilary Fry)

As if their great bone-spongey beaks were too heavy,
A party of Grey Hornbills flops overhead
Through the hot, humid air. These are on migration—
('Well, you tell me where,' the zoologist said)—

They emit high, whining, almost gull-like cries,
Seeming, someone remarks, as if they were mass-produced
Off the production-line of an inferior factory.
But this is not apt. Has it not been deduced

The grotesque Hornbill stems from an ancient race
By the fossil testimony of a small, stony word,
Petrified bone-fragment in alluvial clay?
Look again, you witness a prehistoric bird;

On miocene and pliocene landscapes has gazed
The cold, saurian, humanly eyelashed eye,
Which looks out now over the airfield,
Where forms of camels—not incongruous—stray.

And ceremonial trumpets welcome the guest who comes
By Comet or Viscount, out of the modern century;
The place is not distant from the mediaeval walls,
Nor the satellite-tracking station (Project Mercury).

Here unashamed, anthropomorphic gods send rain;
And dawn, like history, flames a violent birth,
Out of a night with crickets and toads articulate,
For black bodies pushing ground-nuts into the red earth.

1964

THE WATCHMAN'S FLUTE

(Kano)

Through the Nigerian night the Tuareg watchman,
Ferociously armed with sword, daggers and whip,
Intermittently blows his flute—a piece of piping
Bored with five holes: to pass the time—

To ward off tedium, and perhaps
Lurking malignant ghosts that always throng
This ambient, African darkness:

Infinite rhythmical variations
On a simple tetrachord, with a recurrent pedal point—
Libyan music, antique—as Orpheus
Cajoled the powers of Hell, made them disgorge
Eurydice—to him she was love
(Her jurisdiction be wide).

Those deliquescent forms shrink back
To hollow pits of non-entity:
Music implies an order—light,
Particles in regular motion,
The first articulate Word.

May my lips likewise
Mould such melodious mouthfuls still, amid
The European, the twentieth-century tediums:
We too are haunted, we are in the dark.

HOMAGE TO J. S. BACH

It is good just to think about Johann Sebastian
Bach, grinding away like the mills of God,
Producing masterpieces, and legitimate children—
Twenty-one in all—and earning his bread

Instructing choirboys to sing their *ut re mi*,
Provincial and obscure. When Fame's trumpets told
Of Handel displaying magnificent wings of melody,
Setting the waters of Thames on fire with gold,

Old Bach's music did not seem to the point:
He groped in the Gothic vaults of polyphony,
Labouring pedantic miracles of counterpoint.
They did not know that the order of eternity

Transfiguring the order of the Age of Reason,
The timeless accents of super-celestial harmonies,
Filtered into time through that stupendous brain.
It was the dancing angels in their hierarchies,

Teaching at the heart of Reason that Passion existed,
And at the heart of Passion a Crucifixion,
Or when the great waves of his *Sanctus* lifted
The blind art of music into a blinding vision.

IN PRAISE OF JOHN MILTON

On the three-hundredth anniversary of his death 1974

I frame this paean
For the republican
Poet, John Milton,
    Who had skill to sing
Of the super-sensual—
Those fields celestial
Where powers archangelical
    Sweep by on bright wing,

And the darkness visible
Where the final and total
Perversion of the will
    Finds out its own place:
The arrogant tyranny
Of the false democracy
Issuing in the cacophony
    Of a serpent's hiss.

For his is the voice
Of the moral choice—
Whether in the ways
    Of that wandering wood,
Where Comus and his rout
Go about and about,
With bestial shout,
    To seduce if they could,

Or through the verse
By the Laureate hearse,
When the blind fury's shears
    Have slit—to renew
The resolution,
Affirm the vocation,
While the road leads on
    To pastures new;

But that road goes
To the wilderness,
Where the solitariness
  Of the Human Being
Confronts the temptation
Of the Negation,
In confutation
  Of its gainsaying.

It leads to the lands
Of the Philistine bands,
Where a blind man grinds
  In Satanic mills,
Till in power of the truth
He puts forth his strength
And brings down, at length,
  Their house of idols.

As in Eden's bower,
At our midnight hour
The toad at the ear
  Corrupts even the dream;
Life's tree is the haunt
Of the cormorant
Of malign intent,
  Polluted Life's stream:

John Milton, who cast
Three centuries past
Your body to the dust
  Consigned—re-tune
The organs of your praise,
Sound forth to our days,
And justify the ways
  Of Man to Man.

ST MICHAEL AND THE DRAGON

'Who is like God?'—the cosmic war-cry redounds
Through vacant space and clouds of tenuous dust
From galaxy to spinning galaxy
(O the bright spears, O the swift lightning's falchion!).
Unknown Energies muster their squadrons, while
The shadowy Delusion sinks
In wreathed and coiled disorder down,
Shrinks to its own black hole.

CHRISTUS NATUS EST

'Christus natus est!'—it was the Cock's carol
Into the darkness, prefiguring a betrayal.

'Quando?'—the Duck's call is harsh,
Sounding from the reeds of a desolate marsh.

'In hac nocte.'—that voice was the Raven's,
Boding into Man's castle the fatal entrance.

'Ubi?'—it was the Ox that spoke:
We kick against the pricks, we are under the yoke.

'Bethlehem!'—the Lamb, kept for slaughter, said:
God has taken flesh in the House of Bread.

THE GIFTS

Three kings stood before the manger—
And one with a black face—
Holding boxes. Out of the first box,
In bright armour, the spirit of gold
Jumped, a fiery gnome:
'I come from the black mine. I have cheated and corrupted,
A slave to tyrants. Lord, have mercy—
A sign of royalty, a medium of exchange,
I glitter and play in your service.'

Out of the second box streamed forth
In smoke, the spirit of frankincense:
'Before a thousand idolatrous shrines
I've danced my swirling and indefinite dance.
Christ, have mercy—Now at your altar
I burn and sweat myself away in prayer.'

With a rustle of leaves, out of the third box
The spirit of myrrh: 'A bitter herb of the earth,
One of the tares watered by Adam's tears
And mingled with his bread. Lord have mercy—
Making the taste of death
Medicinal, preservative.'

GOLGOTHA

In the middle of the world, in the centre
Of the polluted heart of man, a midden;
A stake stemmed in the rubbish.

From lipless jaws, Adam's skull
Gasped up through the garbage:
'I lie in the discarded dross of history,
Ground down again to the red dust,
The obliterated image. Create me.'

From lips cracked with thirst, the voice
That sounded once over the billows of chaos
When the royal banners advanced, replied through the
                                    smother of dark:
'All is accomplished, all is made new, and look—
All things, once more, are good.'

Then, with a loud cry, exhaled His spirit.

PENTECOST 1975

Courageously
Carols of ouzel and tomtit blossom
To the unseasonable Nor'easter; rose of summer,
Apple and ear of harvest, slumber
Numb in the crude bud.

O crystal Dove, you too
Like Ross's gull sometimes migrate
Northward into the Arctic winter: shake
Out of your snowy wings
Sparkles of frost-fire down,
Vivificator, into the clay-cold heart.

BROKEN LYRES

Demosthenes, mouth filled with pebbles,
Shouts into the storm-wind;

For blind Homer, sunlight glances
On seawave, bronze of armament;

For the eyes of Milton blazes
Celestial Jerusalem;

For Joyce, in unflinching detail,
A dearer and dirtier city;

Uncharted labyrinths of sound
In the silent skull of Beethoven.

The twisted, the unloved bodies—
Leopardi, Pope—

Are broken lyres, are shattered flutes,
For the triumphant spirit

That soars in Eternity's dawn
Like an uncaged skylark.

A FEW STROKES ON THE SAND

Old men, as they grow older, grow the more garrulous,
Drivelling *temporis acta* into their beards,
Argumentative, theoretical, diffuse.

With the poet, not so. One learns
To be spare of words; to make cold thrusts
Into the frosty air that comes.

The final message—a few strokes on the sand;
A bird's footprints running to take off
Into the adverse wind.

FOR A PLATONIST ON HER BIRTHDAY

The further on in time we move,
Here, as through a tangled grove,
In shifting moonlight (each a shade
By shadows fitfully betrayed)
The closer to eternity—that bright
Undifferentiated light.
Yet, stripped of their corporeal dress,
Those alone, who learned to bless,
In time, beneath time-measuring stars,
All the minute particulars,
Can bear that shrivelling radiance:
And then we may begin to dance.

Accept my words—they cannot reach
What Plato and Plotinus teach—
Yet also I, perhaps, have known
How unsubstantial is the stone
(Mountains that crumble in an hour),
How real and timeless is the flower.

FOR A CENTENARY

In the twinkling of an eye
A hundred solar years go by—
Or the exhalation of a sigh:

Someone was born, or someone died;
A commonplace. But human pride
Makes this a date to be descried.

Something was snatched away by Fate:
The minor talent, or the great.
We bring our wreaths. We are too late.

Oblivion will not release
The ashes on the mantlepiece,
Nor pomp of Rome, nor charm of Greece.

17.7.65

CELEBRATION FOR A BIRTH

(S. J. W., born 23 December 1967)

Indifferent weather
She has brought with her,
Sour sleet, together
    With a North-East wind;
While influenza,
Like a devil's cadenza,
And the cattle-murrains, are
    Hurled through the land.

I summon with reason
All saints of the season
On this occasion,
    For graces to sue:
St Stephen I inveigle,
And St John the Evangel
With his wide-winged eagle,
    And the Innocents too;

Sylvester, take heed,
Pious Lucian, at need,
To wish her God-speed
    On her pilgrimage here,
And the Three Kings, whose bones
Lie shrined in the stones
Of Augustan Cologne's
    Cathedral floor.

As sisters fatal,
Stand by the cradle,
Good gifts to ladle,
    The nymphs of the streams;
For I will have brought here
The lost Bayswater,
With Westbourne, the daughter
    Of paternal Thames.

They are not seen now,
But in sewers obscene, are
Thralls to Cloacina
    With her garland of mud;
But I will release them,
And of durance ease them,
If it will please them
    To perform this good.

Child, there's no need you
At all should pay heed to
Those who would mislead you,
    If ever they can:
The troubled heads of Greece—
Even great Sophocles,
With 'Not to be born is' (if you please!)
    'The best for man.'

Pagan delusion
And Gentile abusion
Cause the confusion
    Of their careless talk;
And for this sin, lo,
With arms akimbo,
They sit down in Limbo
    In eternal sulk.

For birth is a blessing,
Though there's no guessing
To what sad issues
    Our life may go;
And when Time shall show it,
And you, too, know it,
Say that a poet
    Told you so.

A FORMALITY

In Memoriam T. S. E.

Poetry is a formality: a continual greeting and leave-taking
For all that we encounter between
A darkness and a darkness. Hail and farewell
To the seven-braided spectrum. At dawn, at sunset;
And each particular thing we learn to love
We must learn to do without. Celebrate this;
Poetry is a formality.

Poetry is a formality: with words we clothe
The naked abstract thought, shivering in its shame—
Only with leaves, only with coats of skin? We can do more—
Go brave through the infected winter
Of our condition. Carnival.
Mask yourself, then. Poetry
Is a formality.

Poetry is a formality: to each
His way of speaking. I would emulate rather those
Who countered despair with elegance, emptiness with a
                                                grace.
And one there is now to be valedicted
With requiem. Poetry also? Also poetry is
A formality.

1965

FOR VERNON WATKINS 1906-1967

Lark in your tower of air,
Over the grey Gower,
As from celestial mansions,
Suspend your concatenations,
The glittering links of your song,
Poised upon dew-drenched wing,
For Gower lies songless here:
Song hallows her no more.

Only the desolate call
Of the wide-winged wandering gull
Is uttered; is heard to grieve,
Wave before following wave,
The lament that breaks in the spray—
The requiems of the sea.

But I remember a man,
Courteous, gentle, humane,
With the dignity of Wales;
One whom time now enrolls
Among the eternities
His words could actualize,
When, at midnight, he did his work—
And a skull, a skull in the dark.

LYKE-WAKE DIRGE, 8 SEPTEMBER 1963

This ay night, this ay night,
    Through a dank September gale,
Into the shy ironic starlight
    Fares forth his naked soul.

Carrickfergus and Birmingham mourn,
    Iceland is desolate;
The armed virgin of the Parthenon
    Signifies her regret.

And it's no go the Third Programme,
    No go a First in Greats,
And it's no go the Golden Bough
    For a passport through the gates.

But sit you down and put them on—
    The wit, the eloquence—
A pair of old brogues with silver buckles,
    The gift you did dispense.

To save your bare bone from the crackling thorns,
    Where pot-boiling waters hiss:
O tightrope-walker, that bridge spans
    The black, the banal abyss.

Fare forth then, protestant, undeceived,
    Till you reach that catholic place
Where, amid her ruins, the Church of Ireland
    Pleads, for her children, grace.

AN ELEGY

(Brian Higgins, ob. 8 December 1965)

Even a slovenly diner at life's banquet
Is missed. Now he also has gone:
His senile heart called this young man away,
At a season of Advent, *in mezzo dell' cammin*.

He wore no mask until he wore a plastic one—
And into that he turned aside to weep:
Positioned in Death Row he saw his death approaching,
Though with the merciful face of her brother, Sleep.

Now let the tribal and trans-Tridentine North
Receive the abused and the self-abused body,
His church pronounce—a mathematically-meaningless
                                                    formula;
The lamp-post that he leaned against is lonely—

It is the guttering light of English poetry. Your muddied
Locks, O nymphs of broad-mouthed Humber, let down,
Who once washed the feet of Andrew Marvell:
Here is another poet that you must mourn.

AT BONCHURCH

(For Maurice Carpenter)

A grasshopper perched on Swinburne's tomb,
Squinnying with eyes like garnets, fiddling his jade-green
                                                    wings:
'Where is the Lesbian melilot, where the singers?
Nuns look after this place now; they ask
Embarrassed pilgrims to kneel down
And say a prayer for my soul. They shouldn't worry—
I have escaped out of the paper-cage,
And skip by coigns of the sea, muse-crazed as always,
But tipsy only, alas,
On non-alcoholic dew that distills before sunrise.'

CAMILLE SAINT-SAENS

The music came
As easy and as elegant as apples
For this, it seems, unloved, unloving man.

The nostrils of his enormous nose
Twitched, in scorn and anger
For the incompetent and the importunate.

The sugar softness of the wedding-cake
Was bait, to draw men down
Into the turning wheel, the grinding mill.

Women enslaved—were Omphale
And were Delilah; women betrayed their children.

And so he fled—to find the desolation
Of affluent hotel rooms, the icy desert
Of a continuing triumph,
And a State Funeral's final emptiness.

Only the animals
Were worthy to be loved, and sported
Through a perpetual carnival
In the lost playground of his innocence.

WINTER IN ILLYRIA

The fountain is choked, yellow leaves
Drift on the broken pavement.
(*'And the rain it raineth'*)

A white peacock
Screams from a windraked arbour.
(*'Come away, Death.'*)

Remembered echoes—echoes of lute-strings,
Echoes of drunken singing.
(*'By swaggering could I never thrive.'*)

Cries of a tormented man, shamed
In a darkened room.
(*'Carry his water to the wise woman!'*)

He left feckless Illyria, changed
His name, enlisted in the army
(*'I'll be revenged on the whole pack of you'*)

In the neighbouring state of Venice, rose to the rank of
                                                    Ancient,
Personal assistant to the General.
(*'Put money in thy purse.'*)

GODSTOW

Rose of the world, corrupted rose—
About and about the maze-path goes:

A thread of silk is caught in his spur,
A spider's clue for Eleanor—

Uprooted rose of Aquitaine
(The poets are singing to England's queen).

The dagger, the green juice in the bowl,
The toads are sucking the breasts of my soul.

And up in arms, they are marching on—
Sodomite Richard and lackland John.

At Trinity-tide the rose is in bloom
For the priest who reigns from his crusted tomb.

And Ireland is up in arms, and curses
The English laws and the English verses.

Plantagenet turns his face to the wall:
'But where is the fairest rose of all?'

SESTINA

The fountain that goes up with plumes of laughter
Comes down with tears, with rainbows and with pearls;
Within dark leaves the gilt and painted pheasant
Perches and preens, as if estranged from terror;
Nor summer knows that her own funeral
She is forever, pyre of her own roses.

Yet the black shadows dodge among the roses
With little jets of chill malicious laughter—
They who are dressed as for a funeral,
Black in their silks, sewn with a few small pearls
But their thin hands are crook'd (I note with terror)
To wring the heart's neck like a pinioned pheasant.

The peacock and the gold and silver pheasant
Down alleyways of peonies and roses
Strut, still as if this place harboured no terror,
And all the green lawns echoing with their laughter,
Children thread daisy-chains, and think them pearls—
Alas, they thread their days for funeral.

They bear a dead mouse to its funeral,
And a plumed mourner is the garden's pheasant
As on the stamped-down turf they scatter roses
Which, when dusk falls, softly the night dew pearls;
Yet with the night there comes a pause to laughter,
And with the dew a sudden hint of terror.

And one may lie awake all night in terror—
As through that darkness goes a funeral,
And in his ears a bitter savage laughter;
He waits for dawn, the loud crow of the pheasant;
From grey to gold and crimson turn the roses
As from their leaves they shed a thousand pearls.

Oh no, not gifts of opals nor of pearls
Nor gold will bribe those ministers of terror
Nor stay their hands that wither all time's roses
And lead the bright world to its funeral,
That shoot down love like a high-flying pheasant
And stifle in the throat our songs and laughter.

Then live with laughter, feed your eyes on pearls
And dine on wine, on pheasant?—think no terror
Before the funeral and the death-pale roses.

THE BEAST

The red and ravaged centre of the opening rose
To the green, gold chafer is assigned;
To lion and wolf the fearful, flying game
On the mountains, in the forests;

The lamprey slowly eats into the fish's entrails; for the leech
The warm and dripping blood;
For whale and oyster the invisible swarms of the sea
They delicately filter:

Each in its kind content. Yet there's one beast
Not populations of earth, sea and sky,
The elements themselves, sun, moon and hosting stars,
Can ever feed—nor yet the heart of Man,

Its ordinary prey, and couching place.

MEDITERRANEAN SPRING

Already the field, fair with leaves, in her fruitful bringing
to birth
Flowers with roses, as they break forth from their buds.
Already on the poising cypress boughs, the cicada,
Muse-crazed, soothes him who binds the sheaves.
A careful parent, the martin has built her house under the
eaves,
Sheltering her progeny within her mud-formed chambers.
Now the sea drowses, through fair days warming into
Zephyr-delighting
Calm its ship-bearing broad expanse;
No longer rushing down on the vessels' high-built poops,
Or throwing up spume upon the line of breakers.
Sailor, to Priapus, lord of the sea and bringer to port,
Sacrifice a bloomy collop of squid or mullet,
Or a cuckoo-wrasse, with fire upon his altars—
Fare forth, untrembling, to the Ionian bounds.

from the Greek of Theaetetus Scholasticus

THE SCRIBE'S RETIREMENT

A lead disc composed of black stuff for marking,
A ruler, the officer who kept the lines straight,
The holder of the stream of black writing ink,
His well-cut pens split at the top,
An abrasive stone which regulates the worn-down pens,
To give definition to the characters when they are rough,
His penknife, a broad pointed metal spear—
These things, the tools of his trade, dedicates
Menedemus, on his retirement, his old eyes growing dim,
To Hermes. Take care of your craftsman.

from the Greek of Damocharis

CHARIXENUS

To the triple goddess of Amarynthus
Charixenus made this threefold dedication—
For the shorn-off locks he had in his youthful time,
Together with his beautiful cicada hair-slide;
An ox likewise sprinkled with lustral water.
The boy gleams like a star, having shed as a horse does
His downy foal's coat.

from the Greek of Theodoridas

IN RETURN FOR THE GIFT OF A POMANDER

(To Cathy Tither)

I am not that butcher's son
    Of Ipswich, the proud Cardinal,
Detesting so the common run,
    He could not pass among them all
Without an orange stuffed with cloves
    Clutched in his white, ringed hands, to quench
The breath of those plebeian droves,
    Their stockfish, leek, and garlic stench;
Though some, who do not love me much,
    Might say I am no democrat,
And that my attitudes are such—
    We will not argue about that:
But I affirm the gift you bring
    Discreetly with my togs shall go,
The night-marauder's silken wing
    To avaunt—although, indeed, we know
There's no sublunary gear
But moth and rust corrupt it here.

The fragrance of a generous thought
Remains. And that cannot be bought.

THE BLAMELESS AETHIOPIANS

My Muse is away dining
With the blameless Aethiopians:
When an Immortal cannot be contacted Homer says
That is where she is.

The blameless anecdotes she formerly
Retailed to me, are whispered
Into an Aethiopian's
Jewel-studded ear.

On Aethiopian mountains
The plantain-eater hoots from the plantain tree:
Has she forgotten the English missel-thrush?

She feasts on Aethiopian delicacies,
And I could only offer her
Braised neck of lamb with carrots.

I do not really blame
The Aethiopians. In love
It takes two to make a silence.

AFTER SAPPHO

Moonset.   Starset.

Midnight.   Time goes.   I lie

Alone.

TO A POET A THOUSAND YEARS HENCE

I who am dead a thousand years
And wrote this crabbed post-classic screed
Transmit it to you—though with doubts
That you possess the skill to read,

Who, with your pink, mutated eyes,
Crouched in the radioactive swamp,
Beneath a leaking shelter, scan
These lines beside a flickering lamp;

Or in some plastic paradise
Of pointless gadgets, if you dwell,
And finding all your wants supplied
Do not suspect it may be Hell.

But does our art of words survive—
Do bards within that swamp rehearse
Tales of the twentieth century,
Nostalgic, in rude epic verse?

Or do computers churn it out—
In lieu of songs of War and Love,
Neat slogans by the State endorsed
And prayers to *Them*, who sit above?

How shall we conquer?—all our pride
Fades like a summer sunset's glow:
Who will read me when I am gone—
For who reads Elroy Flecker now?

Unless, dear poet, you were born,
Like me, a deal behind your time,
There is no reason you should read,
And much less understand, this rhyme.

FROM AN ECCLESIASTICAL CHRONICLE

In the year of Our Lord two thousand one hundred and
                                                    seven,
The first electronic computer
Was appointed to a bishopric in the Church of England.
The consecration took place
At a Pontifical High Mass
In the new Cathedral of Stevenage,
In the presence of the Most Reverend
Mother in God, Her Grace Rita,
By Divine Connivance *Cantuar. Archepiscopissa.*

Monsignor Pff-pff (75321/666)
With notable efficiency, tact, and benevolence, presided
For the next three hundred years
Over his diocese. (He had previously worked
In the mission field—rural Dean of Callisto,
One of the satellites of Jupiter.)
After which he was honourably retired,
Only a little rusted, to the Science Museum
In South Kensington—there frequented and loved
By generations of schoolchildren.

As *The Times* remarked on that occasion,
'He stood for the best in the Anglican tradition.':
In indubitable succession, one might say,
From our contemporary Dr ——, of ——.

LETTER TO PETER AVERY

*Fellow of King's College, Cambridge; a dissuasive
against his becoming part of the 'brain drain'*

There is a curious yarn that says,
Remote, in Ancient British days,
King Bladud, he who ruled in Bath,
And early followed technics' path
Soaring on artificial wings
Above that city of hot springs,
Established here, the tale avers,
A knot of grave philosophers,—
Some choicer minds of Attic Greece—
Such as had talked with Socrates,
Or, near the academic grove,
Heard Plato speak the praise of love
Over a symposiac bottle,
Or took a stroll with Aristotle;
I wonder how they found it here,
Exiled to this sharp northern air,
Expounding philosophic truth
To the blue-stained Brythonic youth
Who crouched within their sordid dens
Among the dank, malarial fens.
But this is a vain Gothic dream;
Such are not dreamt by Camus' stream,
Whose waves have learnt the feet to kiss
Of chastely naked Mathesis,
And taught a muddle-headed nation
Those truths which rest on demonstration—
Till Newton, at the apple's fall,
Ordered sun, moon and planets, all,
Marshalled in Heaven's assembly hall.
Yet, counterpoint in stone perfected,
That which the Royal Saint erected,
Still stands—the Royal Saint, indeed!
The feeble last of his bold breed

From Harry of Monmouth, Kate of France.
Rapt in an ineffectual trance,
He did not curb power-hungry lords
Whose hands were ever at their swords;
They set brash roses on their coats,
Fell to, and cut each other's throats.
Yet he found time to plan this fane:
The Middle Ages in their wane
Are here explicit—Nominalism,
Saints, escutcheons, mysticism—
And after, heresy and schism.
Clear ran the stream, by each smooth lawn,
In the brave Humanistic dawn.
Then the Greek tongue was really heard,
And tuneful was the Attic bird
In Spenser's, Milton's, Cowley's ear—
The air they breathed is sacred air;
While Cudworth, Whichcote, Henry More,
Platonic harmonies restore.
Yet soon the channels choked with lumber,
A Whiggish and Bangorian slumber,
And all the academic folly
Which drove poor Gray to leucocholy;
And Wordsworth also here saw '*blind*'
(In my text this is underlined)
'*Authority beat with his staff*
The child that might have led him.'—Laugh?
Is this concerned with times gone by?—
I think the words may still apply.
Poor Cambridge, poor despondent slough,
What leeches hang about her now,
And (no one seems to find it odd)
Tell Modern Man that he's a god;
The truth, I fear, is more unpleasant:
God may be dead, the Devil isn't.
The times, indeed, are getting late,
Yet still is left to cultivate
A garden here, if so you choose:

A garden where the Iranian rose
Casts to the breeze her pouch of musk,
And listens, in the inebriate dusk,
To the persistent nightingale;
The Attic bird tells the same tale.

APOLOGIA OF A PLASTIC GNOME

The Roman in his garden erected
A statue of Priapus, smeared with red ochre,
With a prodigious phallus, resembling
That of his sacred beast, the donkey:
Multi-purposeful—by sympathetic force
Promoting growth of plants, also a scarecrow,
And that enormous member a useful club
For beating off intruders.

And I am his legitimate successor. Unhappily
I've no apparent phallus, but you mark
My hands are in my pockets, and my plastic trousers
Distinctly tight about my plastic crutch. And my tumescent
Scarlet pointed cap's conspicuous enough.

I stand in the garden of Ted & Lynn—
Mr & Mrs Shortwick—636 Subtopia Avenue
Doing the most I can.

They scarcely know the seasons
Whose diet is frozen peas, frozen string beans,
Frozen brussel sprouts and shepherd's pie.
Their sabbath a long lay-in, ritual
Lustration of the motor-car.

I'm posted in the margin of their mind, to hint
Some Power, imaged as human and yet not,
Or else a surrogate, presides
Over the burgeoning of gladiolus,
Crocus, tea-rose, hollyhock, laburnum,
(King Edwards, sprouting broccoli?).

Scorn not, passer-by, the plastic gnome—
Is doing his best.

SEND FOR LORD TIMOTHY

The Squire is in his library. He is rather worried.
Lady Constance has been found stabbed in the locked
Blue Room, clutching in her hand
A fragment of an Egyptian papyrus. His degenerate half-
brother
Is on his way back from New South Wales.
And what was the butler, Glubb,
Doing in the neolithic stone-circle
Up there on the hill, known to the local rustics
From time immemorial as the Nine Lillywhite Boys?
The Vicar is curiously learned
In Renaissance toxicology. A greenish Hottentot,
Armed with a knobkerry, is concealed in the laurel bushes.

Mother Mary Tiresias is in her parlour.
She is rather worried. Sister Mary Josephus
Has been found suffocated in the scriptorium,
Clutching in her hand a somewhat unspeakable
Central American fetish. Why was the little novice,
Sister Agnes, suddenly struck speechless
Walking in the herbarium? The chaplain, Fr O'Goose
Is almost too profoundly read
In the darker aspects of fourth-century neo-Platonism.
An Eskimo, armed with a harpoon
Is lurking in the organ loft.

The Warden of St Phenol's is in his study.
He is rather worried. Professor Ostracoderm
Has been found strangled on one of the Gothic turrets,
Clutching in his hand a patchouli-scented
Lady's chiffon handkerchief.
The brilliant under-graduate they unjustly sent down
Has transmitted an obscure message in Greek elegiacs
All the way from Tashkent. Whom was the Domestic Bursar
Planning to meet in that evil smelling
Riverside tavern? Why was the Senior Fellow,

Old Doctor Mousebracket, locked in among the incunabula?
An aboriginal Philipino pygmy,
Armed with a blow-pipe and poisoned darts, is hiding behind
The statue of Pallas Athene.

A dark cloud of suspicion broods over all. But even now
Lord Timothy Pratincole (the chinless wonder
With a brain like Leonardo's) or Chief Inspector Palefox
(Although a policeman, patently a gentleman,
And with a First in Greats) or that eccentric scholar,
Monsignor Monstrance, alights from the chuffing train,
Has booked a room at the local hostelry
(*The Dragon of Wantley*) and is chatting up Mine Host,
Entirely democratically, noting down
Local rumours and folk-lore.

Now read on. The murderer will be unmasked,
The cloud of guilt dispersed, the church clock stuck at three,
And the year always
Nineteen twenty or thirty something,
Honey for tea, and nothing
Will ever really happen again.

THE FROG AND THE NIGHTINGALE

Hearing a nightingale one evening sing,
A frog from its puddle opined:
'Among those senseless twittering roulades
Occasionally you note
A deep hoarse croaking, which evinces
Definite marks of talent.

Eh me, what a frog is lost in him!'

NATURE RED IN TOOTH AND CLAW

An exercise in identical rhymes

Sighed a certain young lady from Lyons
(While devoured in a wood by some lions);
    'Alas, how I would
    I were out of this wood,
And just lunching quietly at Lyons!'

Replied the grim chief of the lions:
'O unhappy young lady from Lyons,
    We could not, if we would,
    Let you out of this wood;
We are lunching—this wood is our Lyons.'

NOTE: I am of the opinion that the better known European cities and towns should be given their English pronunciation whenever possible. The young lady whose unhappy fate is recorded in these verses was clearly not French, but English. I think she held a teaching position in a girls' school at Lyons, and this unfortunate event occurred while she was on a vacation trip to Morocco.